A Visit to The Doctor

Revised Edition

Blake A Hoena

raintree

a Capstone company — publishers for children

Raintree is an imprint of Capstone Global Library Limited, a
company incorporated in England and Wales having its registered
office at 264 Banbury Road, Oxford, OX2 7DY – Registered company
number: 6695582

www.raintree.co.uk
myorders@raintree.co.uk

Text © Capstone Global Library Limited 2018

Editorial credits
Sarah Bennett, designer; Tracy Cummins, media researcher,
Laura Manthe, production specialist

Photo credits
Capstone Press: Gary Sundermeyer, Cover Left, 7, 11, 13, 17, 19; Getty
Images: Thomas Barwick, 15; iStockphoto: andresr, 21, fotografixx,
9, RichLegg, 5; Shutterstock: amirage, Design Element, PhotoSerg,
Cover Background

Printed and bound in India

ISBN 978 1 4747 5631 0 (hardback)
22 21 20 19 18
10 9 8 7 6 5 4 3 2 1

ISBN 978 1 4747 5641 9 (paperback)
23 22 21 20 19
10 9 8 7 6 5 4 3 2 1

British Library Cataloguing in Publication Data
A full catalogue record for this book is available from the British
Library.

Contents

The doctor's surgery

A doctor's surgery is a busy place to visit. People go to the doctor when they are ill or need a check-up.

People sit in the waiting room.

They wait to see

a doctor or a nurse.

At the doctor's

Office workers keep records

and make appointments.

They file charts and answer

the phones.

Nurses help patients get ready

to see a doctor.

Nurses write down how

much each patient weighs.

Doctors write prescriptions

and read charts.

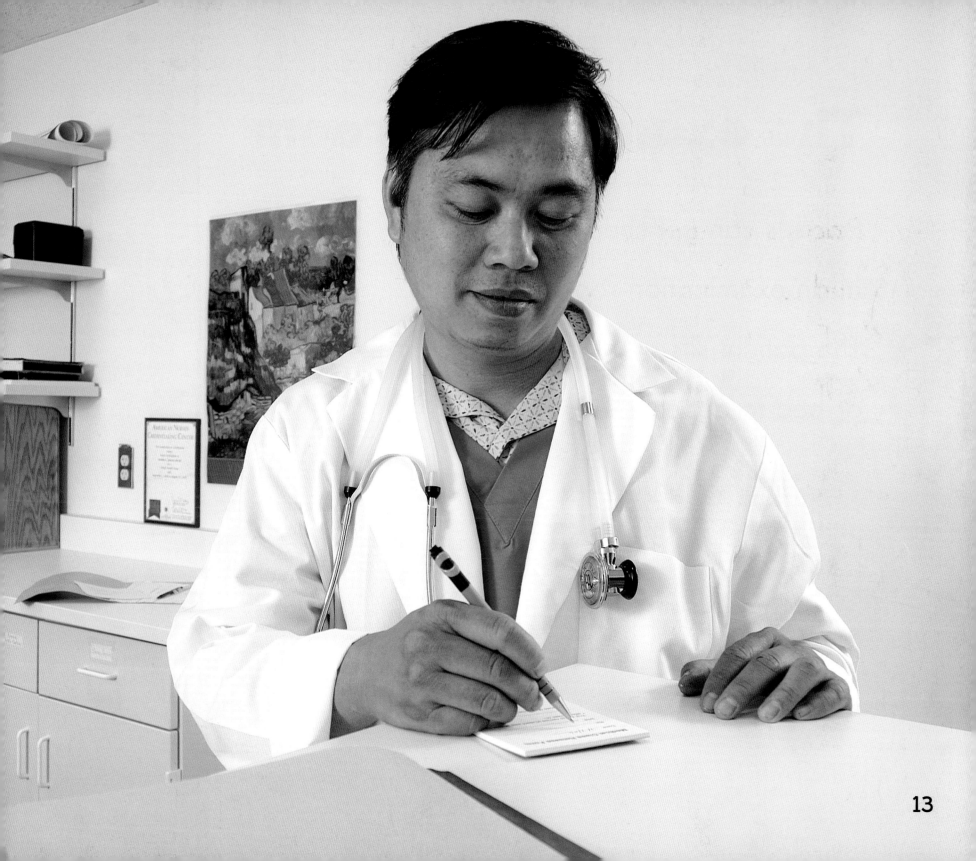

The examination room

Patients can get checked

in an examination room.

The patient sits on a table

or bed to get checked.

Instruments help doctors

and nurses check their patients.

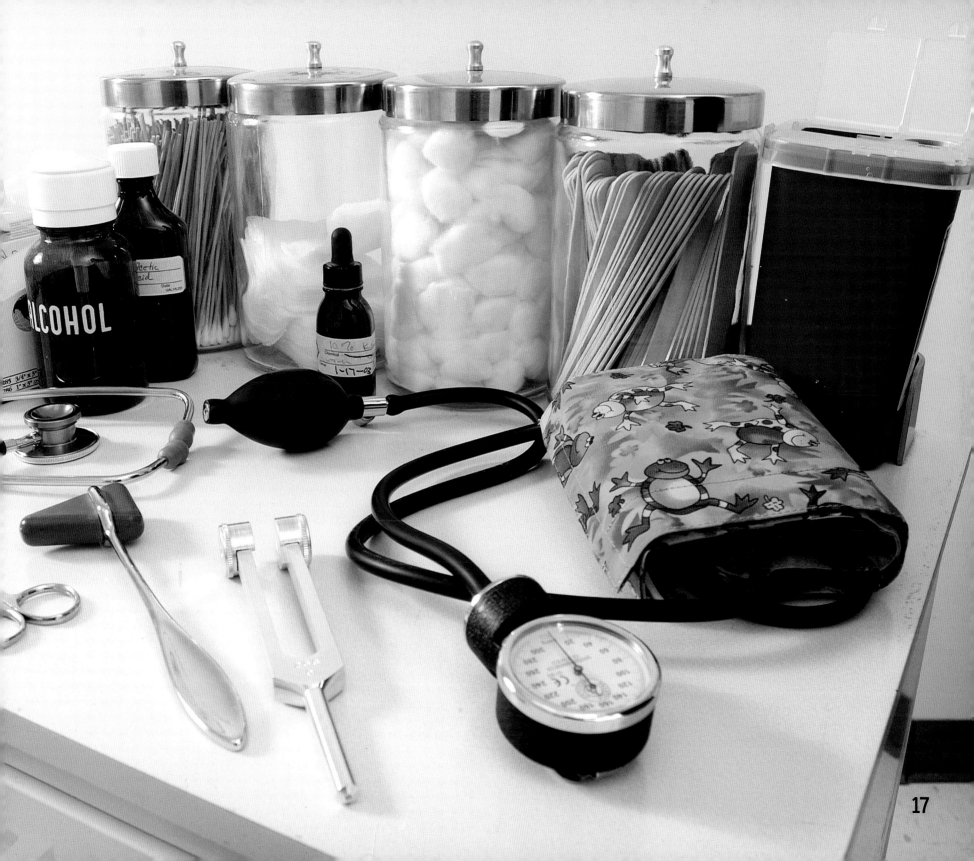

The lab

Lab workers do tests in the lab.
They wear gloves to keep
their hands clean and safe.

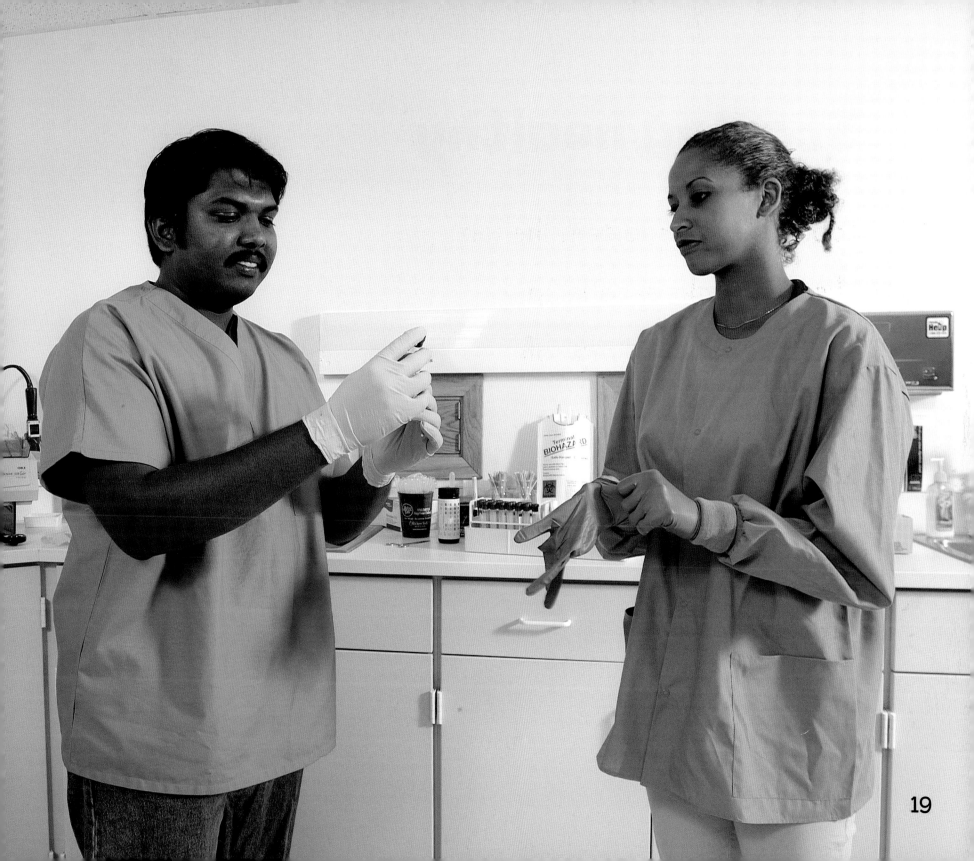

Staying healthy

People visit the doctor
to help them feel better
and stay healthy.

Glossary

appointment arrangement to meet someone at a certain time

chart place where information about a patient is kept; information is added to a chart each time a patient visits the doctor's office

examination room room where doctors and nurses check the health of a patient

instrument medical tool used to examine or treat patients

lab room with equipment that is used to do scientific tests; another word for lab is laboratory

patient person who is cared for by a doctor or a nurse

prescription written order for medicine

Find out more

Books

Doctor (Here to Help) Hannah Phillips, (Franklin Watts, 2017)

My Visit to the Doctor (Reading Roundabout), Paul Humphrey, (Franklin Watts, 2008)

Visit to the Doctor (My First) Eve Marleau, (QED Publishing, 2010)

Websites

www.healthforkids.co.uk
Look at this fun website to find out about healthy eating and how to look after yourself.

www.nhs.uk/change4life-beta/cards
Find out about healthy foods and discover some tasty recipes at this NHS website.

Comprehension questions

1. What do lab workers wear to stay safe?

2. Describe what nurses do.

3. Do you like going to the doctor? Why or why not?

Index